A happy heart
makes the face
cheerful,
but heartache
crushes the spirit.

Proverbs 15:13 NIV

BE HAPPY...

Contents

INTRODUCTION...1
CHAPTER 01..2
　Own Your Own Happiness..2
CHAPTER 02..3
　Challenge Your Own Story..3
CHAPTER 03..4
　Enjoy The Journey...4
CHAPTER 04..5
　Make Relationships Count..5
CHAPTER 05..7
　Balance Work With Play..7

INTRODUCTION

What constitutes happiness for us? It is not surprising that we all still try to find the response, even now, without realizing it, to what can be one of the oldest questions that men have ever posed. In the dictionary, it means *"quality or state of being happy; bliss, contentment; success; good fortune, luck."* It can also be defined as *"a lasting state of fullness, satisfaction, and balance,"* or the meaning of spiritual well-being or inner peace. Regardless of its meaning, one thing is for certain, we all want happiness, whatever happiness might be.

No one will take your joy away from you

John 16:22

In our constant search for it, however, we risk losing "being" in our never-ending quest for happiness tied to "having." Life is made up of "little moments," they say, and enjoyment is found in the "simple things in life." These sayings, in my opinion, can **convey important realities.** We risk getting lost when living just for possessions, and we might not even realize the minor joys along the road. This book lists **five important pillars** to happiness and explains how this constant search might not be a "search" after all.

After all this time, it's still you.

CHAPTER 01

Own Your Own Happiness

The concept that society forces upon us that we must always be happy, that unhappiness is a terrible thing, and that we cannot express it leads to a mistaken pursuit of happiness. Today, people are almost required to be happy, and those who are unhappy are viewed as terrible failures.

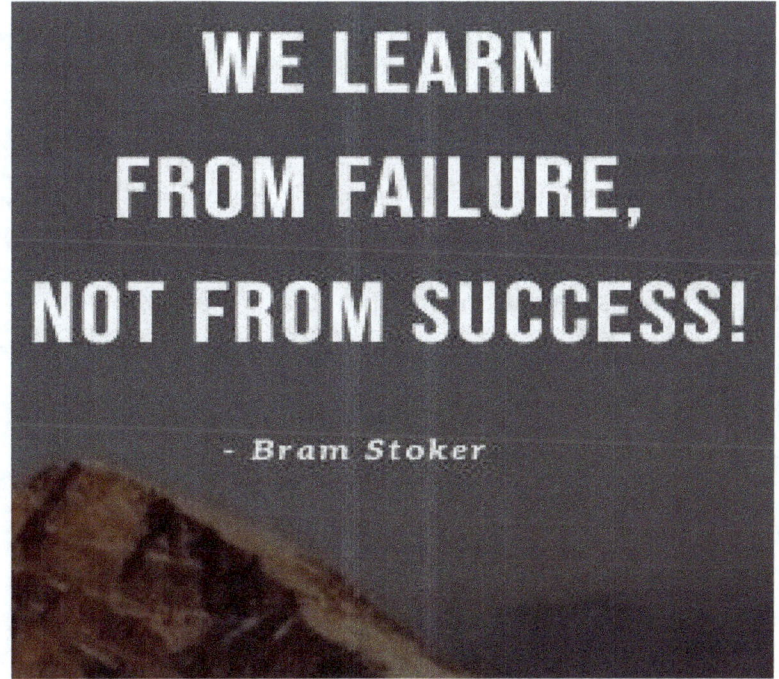

This feeling can eventually develop into depression, the evil of a society that has decided to be happy at all costs. Many of us are even trying too hard to show happiness to others and suffering inside because of it. Happiness is becoming a burden, a terrible source of anxiety.

> "MISTAKES AND PRESSURE ARE INEVITABLE THE SECRET TO GETTING PAST THEM IS TO STAY CALM."

In light of this, we must acknowledge and accept that being unhappy is equally essential. You will make a significant advancement in self-knowledge by confronting sorrow and sadness head-on and pinpointing all of its sources, especially since these difficult times will provide us with the opportunity to pursue our own happiness.

> "The greatest weapon against stress is our ability to choose one thought over another.

But if "having" isn't what it means to be happy, then what's happiness truly about?

According to [Dr. William Barcley](), the key to contentment is "learning to be pleased with what you have," regardless of "having a lot or having little." It's about recognizing that life comprises **everyday good and unpleasant moments** and that each contains wisdom and learning. Difficult and complex, but something to consider.

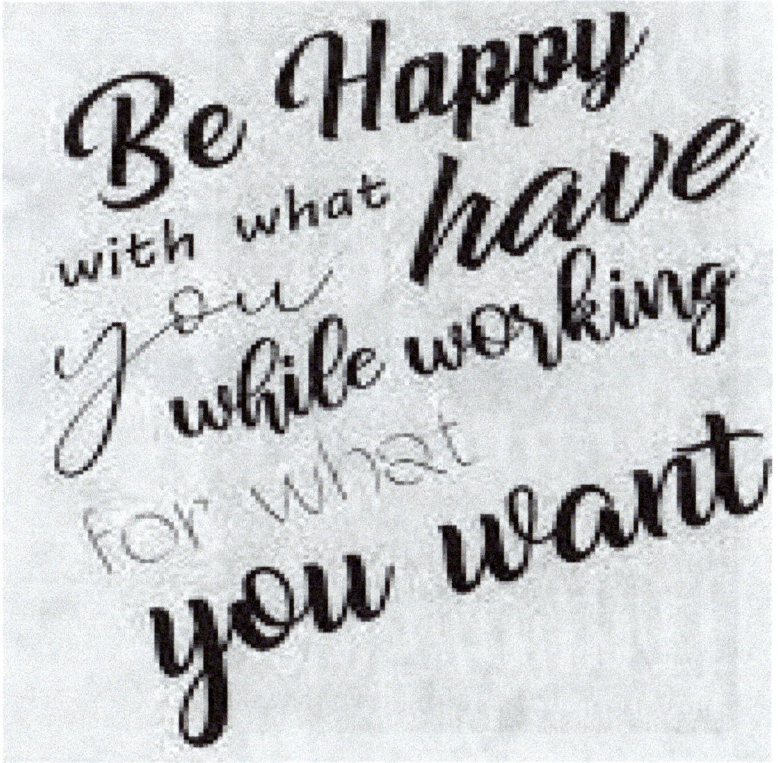

The answer is that there are no formulas for happiness, nor is there a model that we can pass on to others, but one thing is consistent in the lives of individuals who are happy: **they are intimate with themselves**, that is, they are aware of and devoted to their own wishes.

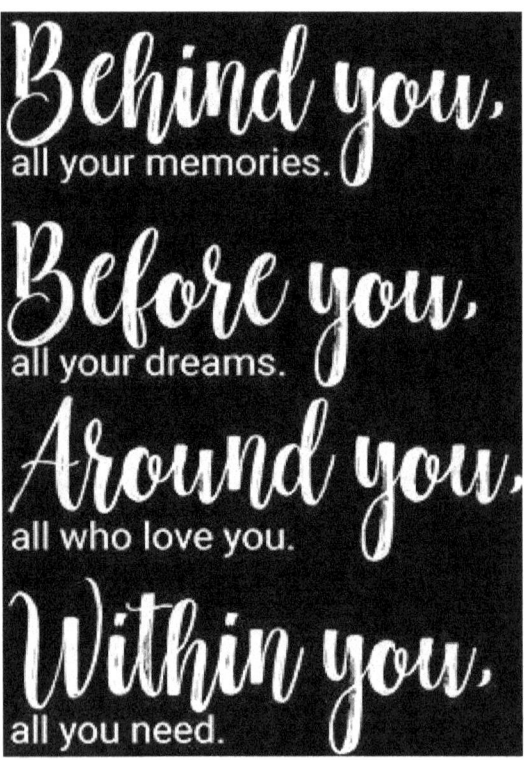

The only way to do it is through self-awareness. Only through it will we be able to discover our wills, boundaries, and all that genuinely makes our hearts vibrate. Those who are able to do so will be able to live with happiness.

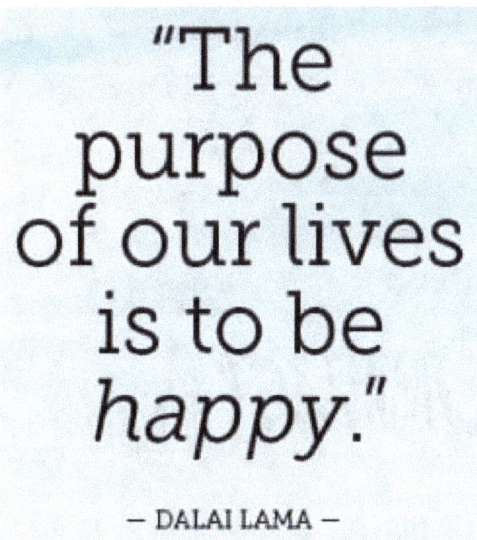

However, all those who are constantly running after happiness or waiting for pleasure to come as if it was an order in a restaurant haven't yet grasped that **happiness doesn't exist somewhere other than within each person**, and joy isn't planned for the future; it may happen right now.

Breathe! Become aware of yourself and make that connection. Find out what actually moves you by feeling it. Just as a beach is made up of microscopic sand grains, happiness may result from enjoying the smallest things in our lives.

CHAPTER 02

Challenge Your Own Story

Turning your focus to yourself and your own story is a brave act that hardly everyone does since it is within ourselves that we discover all the imperfections we perceive in others. It is challenging to realize that we're often judgmental of others even though we have many flaws ourselves.

Fortunately for us, there's a simple solution! It seems as though the instant you become aware of your flaws, they lose power. And I know that by putting it this way, it sounds easy, but this is a process to be worked on for a lifetime. And that's where self-care comes in.

> It's not selfish to love yourself,
> take care of yourself, and make
> your happiness a priority.
> It's necessary.
>
> Mandy Hale

Have you ever considered that you will be your own company for the rest of your life? People will come and go, and whatever happens, in the end, you'll only have yourself. As a result, your priority should be to become a good company for yourself.

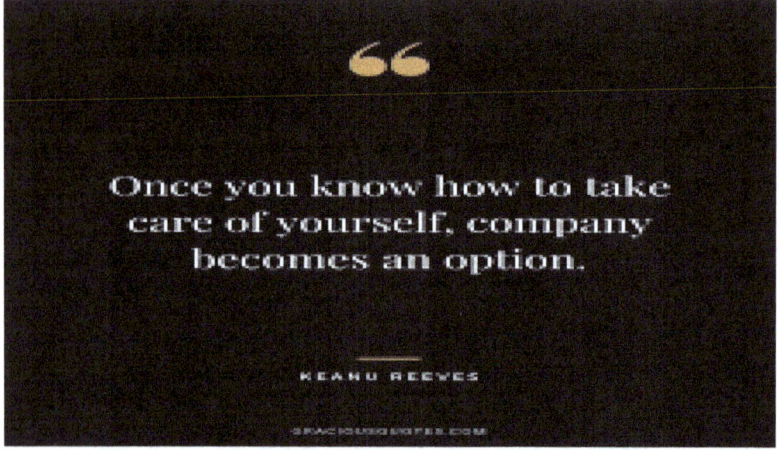

But how? The first step is to acknowledge and admit that you are constantly unable to see happiness in your everyday life. The second is a desire to understand why you feel this way, and the third is realizing there's a solution for everything. It might seem "too obvious," but it is not!

When you are in a difficult circumstance or stressed, I'm sure you picture the worst situations and possibilities, blame yourself, condemn yourself, say negative things to yourself, and in many cases even mask these sentiments with distractions, drinking, social media, or any other types of escape. That causes you to forget about the core problem.

On the other hand, when we give ourselves time and space to listen to what is going on within our heads, **when we welcome ourselves**, listen to each other, and aspire to be our greatest friend, we are planting the finest possible seed inside ourselves.

This practice is really powerful and contagious because you start little, simply trying not to beat yourself up when you make a mistake, and then when you realize that you should love yourself even at the most difficult time and that this attitude can radically transform your day, week, and life.

It's as if we build a nest within ourselves so that no matter what happens in the outer world, we can return to a cozy and warm house at the end of the day. But establishing this nest takes a lot of love, patience, self-care, and self-preservation.

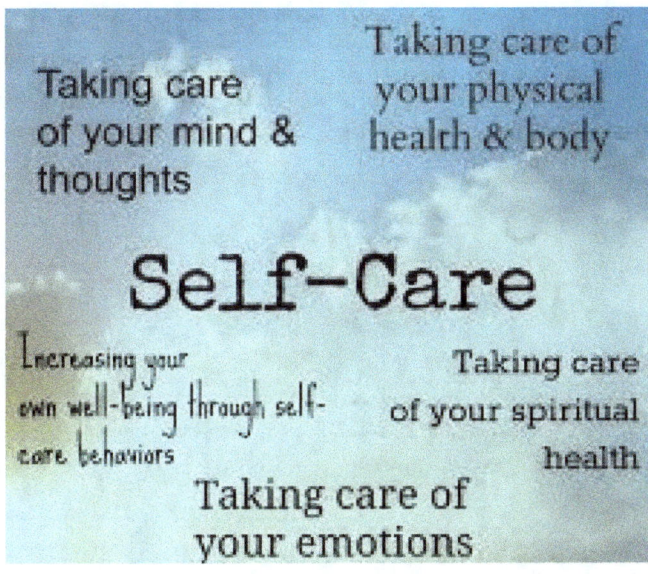

Understand that our lives aren't supposed to be perfect and that, in the end, the world is a mess. Our only hope in life is to clean it up and make it a better place for all of us, but you can't change the exterior without first addressing the internal. We must do better for ourselves!

When we are stressed, unhappy, and anxious, our contribution to the world stagnates, which can lead to mental and physical disorders. So, it's critical to remember that the better we take care of ourselves and stay well, the better we are to those around us, the world we live in, and ultimately ourselves.

> TO FALL IN *love* WITH *yourself* IS THE FIRST SECRET TO *happiness.*
> — ROBERT MORLEY

CHAPTER 03

Enjoy The Journey

As children, we learn to approach practically everything as work that must be completed promptly and successfully. These are merely false beliefs, and our life is much more poetic than that! Simply observing nature for a few minutes can demonstrate this. Just as people say that "life is a school," maybe you're simply in math class and missed recess! Maybe you forgot about mischief, friendships, chatting and laughing, and outings... The good parts of your experience.

You know those vacations where you go through a huge scare that is sometimes frightening at the moment, but after a few days or weeks, you're already telling the experience and having fun? That's how it is in real life. Only you can begin having fun right now! Don't treat self-knowledge and expansion of consciousness as another task on your endless to-do list. Don't make something so precious become a burden!

No result justifies a life without happiness, curiosity, adventure, or pleasure. Don't put pleasure off until you're off duty; work and fun must walk together! Every stage of the journey has its own beauty; appreciate what you are experiencing right now! Are you working hard? Enjoy the laugh with coworkers. Do you have less work? Enjoy the pleasures of relaxation! Are you involved with someone? Enjoy the beauty of sharing! Are you alone? Enjoy the tranquility of solitude! Don't have a car? Enjoy the thrill of discovering your city through new eyes! Are you sick? Enjoy the delight of self-care and see the healing power of the body!

Of course, we can reject and try to change any circumstances that we find unpleasant, but when reality reveals itself and comes to teach or reveal something to us, we have a choice between learning through love or fear—and going with the teacher known as love is always the better option! As you transform your reality and co-create one that has more connection to your soul, **enjoy the journey!**

CHAPTER 04

Make Relationships Count

There was a period when the concept of individualism seemed to be the norm, and uncontrolled consumerism and self-sufficiency were both highly admired. Time has passed, though, and the situation appears to have fully turned around. The concept of togetherness and the notion that no one truly lives alone has started to become stronger, and there's a lot we can learn from it.

Be mindful that being single and living alone are not the same thing. Living alone, in the broadest meaning of the word, refers to much more than just not having or being near one's family. It entails not having friends or anybody you can confide in, communicate with, or socialize with. It refers to solitude in the purest meaning that you can imagine.

However, living is only possible, whether in the sense that happiness is linked to sharing our moments with other people but also to the functioning of a society to which we belong if we're together. Whether you like it or not, life in society is so important that we are trained for it from birth. The first stage is often the family, with childhood activities and school life serving as preparation.

Despite all of this, the concept of "I wish to just be alone" is still prevalent among many individuals, and many take this phrase seriously in all of its meanings. Some people associate the word "alone" with the concept of singleness. Some interpret this as a need to be surrounded by a large number of people, although this is not the case. The only truth is that it is important to remember that **individualism and a sense of belonging must coexist in order to live a fulfilling life.**

Having people around us also makes us happier and healthier, so investing in stable, long-lasting, and happy friendships is thus a healthy and necessary approach to care for our wellness. Naturally, we must be thankful for and cherish our healthy family ties, strong friendships, and the support of a web of relationships we construct throughout our lives.

Because we are absolutely sociable beings, how people see us also shapes who we are. We require the validation of others to influence our ideals and character. If I say something hilarious, for example, I confirm it by seeing the reaction of those around me.

In the end, just as it is clear that a newborn needs other people to provide for all of its needs, it is also true that having a support network - family, friends, a community – even as adults have a huge influence on all aspects of our lives and our search for happiness.

CHAPTER 05

Balance Work With Play

Your career is really important to you; I get it. However, your life is more than simply your job or the organization you work for. There is much more to life than the desk where you sit every day. It's also crucial to take care of your mental health, family, leisure, and hobbies that can offer you joy and relaxation...

When fired, people who become extremely attached to their work are often left with no ground to stand on. Their "life" ends there. But take notes! Your "ground" is your whole life, your trajectory in all aspects (not just your job), your children, your abilities, skills, contributions to the world, and even your religion.

You are a vast cosmos that is not limited to a single component of the whole. Obviously, it is good to produce well and inspire yourself, blessing the task you have today and executing it to the best of your ability. But it isn't the only thing that matters. Know how to maintain emotional strength so that, in times of crisis, you can create, innovate, and have the tenacity and tranquility to reinvent yourself (and, if necessary, re-employ yourself!).

In the end, you'll realize that the greatest personal achievement is sitting at a bar with friends and having a nice beer without thinking about the work you missed today because you were overwhelmed and didn't have time. Go for what makes your heart skip a beat.

Give yourself the privilege to worry about something other than your retirement and mortgage. There are no drawers in coffins, and anything you earn in life will not be taken away when you die. What you take from this life is the **life you lead**.

YOU
—— do ——
YOU

WATCH YOUR THOUGHTS,
FOR THEY BECOME WORDS.

WATCH YOUR WORDS,
FOR THEY BECOME ACTIONS.

WATCH YOUR ACTIONS,
FOR THEY BECOME HABITS.

WATCH YOUR HABITS,
FOR THEY BECOME CHARACTER.

WATCH YOUR CHARACTER,
FOR IT BECOMES YOUR DESTINY.

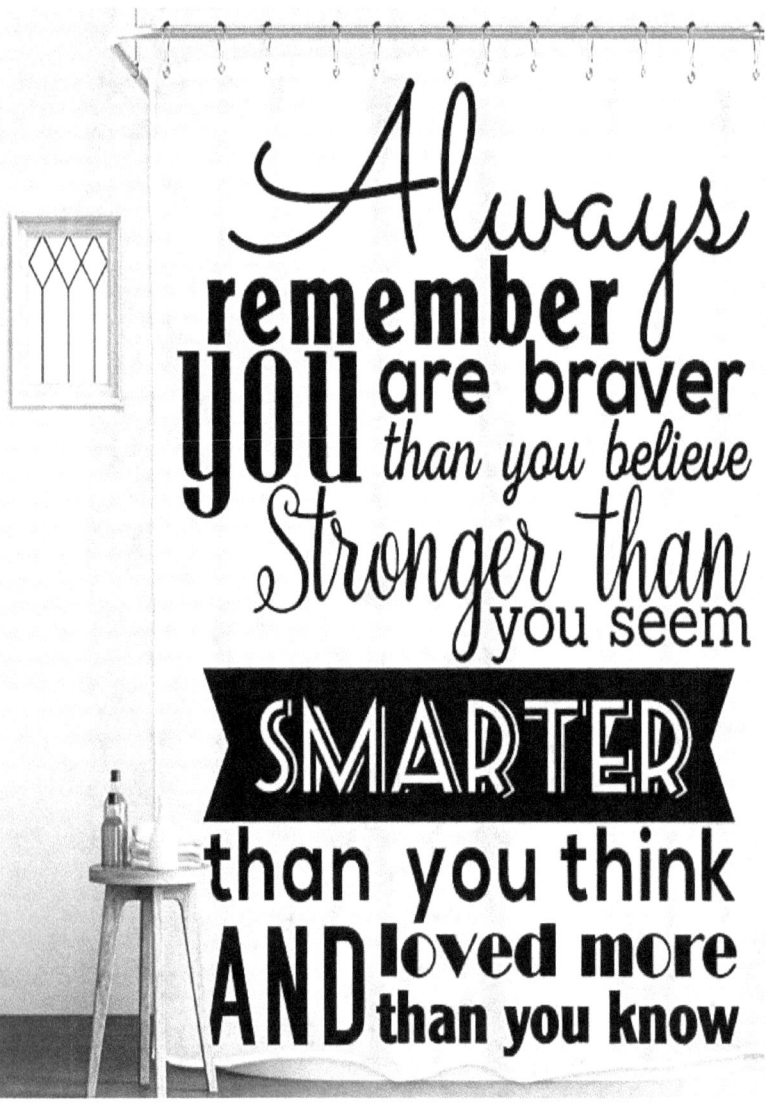

Just be happy
It drives people
Crazy

www.ingramcontent.com/pod-product-compliance
Lightning Source LLC
Chambersburg PA
CBHW070443010526
44118CB00014B/2176